TWITCH FORCE

Also by Michael Redhill

TWITCH
FORCE

POEMS

MICHAEL
REDHILL

ANANSI

Published in Canada in 2019 and the USA in 2019 by House of Anansi Press Inc.
www.houseofanansi.com

House of Anansi Press is committed to protecting our natural environment. As part of our efforts, the interior of this book is printed on paper made from second-growth forests and is acid-free.

23 22 21 20 19   1 2 3 4 5

Library and Archives Canada Cataloguing in Publication

Redhill, Michael, 1966–, author
Twitch force / Michael Redhill.

Poems.
Issued in print and electronic formats.
ISBN 978-1-4870-0620-4 (hardcover).—ISBN 978-1-4870-0618-1 (softcover).—
ISBN 978-1-4870-0619-8 (PDF)

I. Title.

PS8585.E3425T85 2019   C811'.54   C2018-905434-4
                              C2018-905435-2

Library of Congress Control Number: 2018961238

Book design: Alysia Shewchuk

Canada Council   Conseil des Arts   ONTARIO ARTS COUNCIL
for the Arts   du Canada   CONSEIL DES ARTS DE L'ONTARIO
                                      an Ontario government agency
                                      un organisme du gouvernement de l'Ontario

We acknowledge for their financial support of our publishing program the Canada Council for the Arts, the Ontario Arts Council, and the Government of Canada.

Printed and bound in Canada

In memory of Don Coles

CONTENTS

CHEMICAL DROWSING / 25

Vertebrate skeletal muscle functions as a biological motor, converting chemical energy to mechanical energy to generate force and do work that powers movement. An important property of muscle mechanical function is that it is history-dependent, and as such is sensitive to previous muscle activity. An important example of this history-dependence is "force potentiation," defined as the transient increase in isometric twitch force evoked by prior contractile activity.

— Rene Vandenboom, "Force Potentiation in Skeletal Muscle"

ASTRONOMICAL TWILIGHT

ASKEW

I was in the hall mirror all yesterday, the next morning gone.
The grade had steepened, things were sliding off.
Everything looked normal if you held your head funny.

My speech impediment makes others appear bowlegged to me.
Run your tongue over my teeth. Try to talk like that.

Going at it all day hammer and hammer and tong and tong. If I shake this thing
long enough what's inside it will come out. That's what I'm here for.
I paid for the supper and I want the show. I saw my doppelganger

working the coat check and he was already wearing my coat. This was at
Bowles Lunch at Bay and Queen in 1924. Change shape again if the budget allows,

otherwise get busy stacking things. That loud sucking noise you hear
is someone drinking a Coke on the PA. Worrying about the wrong things
doesn't make a sound. Someone in the chorus is laughing! Let's

bring it in. Who got the chalice from the bus?
Who has the sunblock? The life we're working toward

is in this direction, I'm sure of it. Now cover your eyes.

CHEESE SKIPPER

You don't get this kind of fly except in wet Octobers.
They die in their hundreds at night,
drawn by light and killed in it. Their short day

involves reproducing and becoming metaphors.
Their wings are the hooks of open quotes
dried up black on the tabletop. Unsaid things.

The internet sags with advice on how to rid yourself
of them. As in all the best spy novels, it ends
with a turncoat revealing the source: a counteragent

who burrowed into the mould under the sink
and turned on the cloning machine. Come forth
on your feast-day, *Piophila c.* Your soldiers are husks

on something called a kitchen table.

FORMS

All stories are about an absence.
Don't think of one that isn't.
Anomaly is presence, otherwise it's normal.
A single shoe is a useless thing.

Poignant means pregnant, such as when
you don't know if there's another self inside you.
An internal rhythm is often enough
to make it seem like you're there.

The shape of an empty glove is all things to their purpose.
What you believe takes form, surrenders.

Its sewers hold wine now,
the basilica's husk stores collectable LPs.
A pointless wall rings it, that dead
private city where they watched the sea.
Water at the gate, the mountain behind
dependable as a shadow. Mud sixteen metres
deep walled them into the sea. They became
versions of themselves, a fear we share with them.
There was an ivory comb in the pocket
of a young girl. Alone in one of the villas,
I stared at paint that some hand had
laid down, a yellow line on a wall.
I scraped it with a fingernail,
saw the blue wall of yet another life.

I decide to leave the curtains wide open so I can see night fall but you never choose what you're thinking so you're both wrong and the dog is scared of the soundwaves an electric guitar makes and the people who don't remember what happened outnumber us but sound moves out from its source in rippling waves to tell you where you are so sometimes the wrong choice is better for history in the long run like Paul Gauguin in Arles and the sonic range of an electric guitar is around four hundred hertz or about double the human voice.

Thirteen is a magic number so say twelve-year-olds and to fail to fail is to succeed but every culture makes the same food out of slightly different ingredients and some of the stories I tell are untrue but not the one about treating blue balls with Rub A535 and the silence of a dark room seems denser than the same room lit so something has been happening every moment you've been alive and you've forgotten all but one percent of it and researchers report unseen things may have slightly less mass than seen things and five is magic too.

Vanity is a sign of life expressed in organic symbols and if they sold human conditioner I'd buy it but the closest you get to another person is reading notes they've written in their books and cold is the absence of heat only if you happen to be hot so being gets in the way of happiness is my experience and sex is not a human right like safe shelter but they should put it in the water anyway and you shouldn't underestimate the power of touch and you're the last of something and atoms don't accelerate they get excited.

Everyone hears voices you're hearing one now and I never breathe properly when I'm typing but fifteen minutes of foreplay suggests you're not really a serious person so I might be making you up as I go along and eating an egg is a teleological act but drowning is more literary than plane crashes and a beloved cookbook gets filthy but nothing you say or hear or think is the actual truth and possibly the best things only happen in minor keys but if you ever scream for your life you'll hear yourself from fifty thousand years ago.

That feeling you have that something is terribly wrong is accurate and your books smell like all your houses but there are people who have read *Lependu* and people who don't own sports cards but I use the daily news as neural room tone and I'm an addict on four internet forums and the brain of a bullfrog is about the same size as a fetus at nine weeks but even the primitive brain thinks this is really happening and taxonomy is playing favourites but why I believe what I believe will be announced later although I mean much later.

CHARLATANS

I'm a bit of a charlatan, but then again, so am I.
I don't fear this symmetry, it saves time
better than changing one's shirt or club.
Falsehoods flash like bulbs and go dark.

In some places (think Vegas) surgical enlargements
are two for one. The fun lies in seeing
how far you can go off true and stay yourself.
Now, *that* shit deepens like a coastal shelf.

Down south, they think the winter snow
an artifice, a cover, that there are sheets of it
built up to hide some colourful truth. Those in the know
know there's nothing but snow, tho.

False-bottomed boats in man-made lagoons
show you evidence of what came before. Forfeit
and evolution: an archeology of striving. Eons
and miles of cold are dressed as something.

where is the good information   am I too tired for drinks?
   what to do if you can't stop crying

   how not to look threatening   cheap flights
best treatment for personal itching   will it be fun?

how to become more permeable   I feel lucky   explain holographic universe
where is the hidden keyboard?   correct spelling of ecclessiasticcal

tantric cooking   cheap flights   nuclear capacity   big breasts
         can I electrocute myself with a 9-volt battery?   work from home

indelible ink removal   laser tattoo   best way to slice a leg of lamb
introductory remarks   ancestor simulation   cheap flights

did you mean *peristalsis*?

LES INSOMNIAQUES S'AMUSENT

You have to open a box of old letters carefully.
The lid comes off with an exhale.
Torn counties from the Railway

and Postal Map of the Dominion
of Canada (1881), found in hoarded ephemera.

held-in breath. Silverworm tracks
make paper labyrinths. A Jane
I barely knew sent a photo and a manuscript.

The vectors of insomnia pull in both directions
with equal force: opiate lure and arrow of terror,

you could almost levitate but you're not up for it.
The old townships are unlicensed. Asphodel
no longer exists, it's merged with Norwood.

We're already speaking fondly of yesterweek:
remember when it didn't suck? Drinking from

your mother's flesh, this thought formed:
Ah, but for when I was three hours old.
What I wouldn't do for your wet, velvety

emptiness, Mother. The dark I'm staring through
flickers like shutters and the sirens aren't helping.

I can hear the dog trembling in his bed.

SEQUELAE

Self is inflamed by pain.

Everyone knows it's white.

Matter makes a dire osmosis.

This is happening. Now I get it!

Ghost is impaired all by itself.

Inferred reefer.

There are a lot of ways out and some of them are.

Dagger nations dagger by nature.

Speeding toward us.

Before the internet, I wore ugly vests.

I'm down with gravity and up with people.

Most of the time I believe I'm a man in a man's body.

I'm one of sixteen personalities.

I consent to this.

She harangues the bellman from the comfort of her personal
motorized device, wants to be rounded up to a buffet comp,
wants to know if the fish is done kosher-style. Her husband
in his Dolphins hat holds his flip-phone to his skull,
she nibbles his other ear. *Later,* she says, *you can fuck me*
with your stump. You don't want to know

what happened to the guest who fell into the koi pond
in the Serenity Garden. On YouTube you can watch
carp debride a piglet in nine seconds flat.
Take the roof off any large habitation and we resemble
every other kind of scurrying. Grain renews the workforce
through early death so people like us
can PVR *Shark Week* and then watch it
the week after *Shark Week.* That's the paleo diet, complete
with breathing apparatus. At the slot bays

they've programmed meat to push buttons. All
the sugar is free. Miss America scratches her bonus card
tongue wedged in her cheek. Her husband is still on his phone:
Those clients go through me! Don't let them call you,
tell them to call me! and he snaps the conversation off.
Then she's gone and he slipstreams in her wake: two living things.

A man doffs his cap to the streetcar,
smiles at Richard Baños, who operates
the camera-machine. He balances
a silver box, cantilevered handles tipped in wood.
Leaning out he's an early modern, hurdy-gurdying.
The Spanish-made steel grinding beneath the streetcar
whistles (I'm thinking) toward the Barcelona hills.

The people who wave to the camera are gone.
Their bodies inaugurate a species
that waves to itself. The sped-up film
makes them look the way everything feels.

On the Avinguda de la República Argentina
a man strides out of treeshadow
to get a better look at me. I shake his hand
a hundred and eleven years ago.

Bury a tomato seedling up to its neck and
its body will speed into the dirt, a chaos
of becoming. Your hair along the dark

pillowcase in the dark room. Into the unknown,
multiples of sporelike futures branch.
Your whole life is spent jarring atoms loose,

trying to deliver your person to someone else.
Therefore: resistance is erotic. The seedlings
peek out of their wet holes

and reinvent themselves. The taproot
of the Black Trifele can reach a depth
of twenty-two inches. *Like a beautiful*

mahogany-colored Bartlett pear with greenish shoulders.
From room to room in houses all along the street
a strong reaching under the soil,

disorder of roots. Plants spaced two feet apart
may eventually touch. Maturity
in six weeks. Collect them, cut them

into centimetre-wide black discs, apply salt.
They look like gears of different sizes
from a machine made of dirt.

Death-adoring fruit, shadowy kilojoules,
a dozen calories in a cap, not enough
to fire a thought. They crop up like *ahems* in the forest
anaemic or glowing bubon black and brown,
the brown of human flesh or hair.
Flattened there, eons flowing,
decaying portfolio, a burp in the damp.

They adapt to the dead and thrive,
stencil ghosts in trees, remake
themselves in a frill of dark amnion.
Congress with the living,
almighty caul of hyphae.

(The fragrant clitocybe is
sometimes slighty depressed.)

Trumpet of Death!

Dark villages, asleep for hours now,
sweep by, candles flickering in windows.
I drive Main Street, Magellan under the moon,
the gas station shut until morning, the road
silenced by snow. Trumansburg, Covert,
Ovid. Through silent towns, the night lights up.
In the washed-out skies of my childhood,
sometimes a vibrant star would urge itself
over the rooftops or else we'd have to go
to the planetarium and gape at the universe in a bowl.
But here there's only the scattered salt
of the starblown night, thrown for luck.
The cupolaed farmhouses wheel by cloaked
in faint light, their basements reliquaries of war,
bones and scuppered backhoes lying under corn.
Later, standing at a lookout over dark Cayuga,
the long lake seems like a tear in the world.

Shades of darkness, prenight blueblack.
It's hard to see in civil twilight. The glow in the sky drains
below the horizon and grades of dark and pitch
mount to a dome of stars. I have to squint
to make you out, to see your dark lines
against this slate of nothing.

Constellation of apricots, windfall,
spent sugar. After months of flower,
hard green buds showed and the fruit thickened
to sunlight and halo. Starting in July
the wind brought them down.

The night of the celebration, people
gathered in a park to watch fireworks.
Smoke drifted over the fences, roman candles
sent balls of orange light to the horizon. Shake
and sizzle, the empty banging of the stars.

Made acceptance speeches, repelled
the Nazi scourge, had sex with lesbians,
convinced parents to keep the dog (age six),
visualized the tomatoes ripening, saw her
for the first time again, present at Dieppe,
shouted *help is coming, hold on!* plea
bargained, filibustered, sneered
at Kitty Hawk. Lay on my back and
was an oyster at Leucate Plage, signed
that kid's cast, watched the car
hit someone else's child in Berga,
opened the envelope, gave
the eulogy (whole room wept), remembered
the lost perogy recipe that called
for cottage cheese. Turned over again —
smear of the red-numbered clock —
designed book covers, tucked in under a left
and put down Chuck Liddell, caught
bullfrogs in the muck at the edge of Pine Lake,
brought back the smell of blueberry buns
from the Open Window Bakery, drove
the narrowing roads north. In my hand
I held the closed head of a milkweed pod
and peeled it back to white

Bitterly sane, I can't leave myself. No drug
pulls me out of my animal. I want to be
counted without my proxy, that stalking
shambles melting like a window.
My body's obsessive evanescence is a turn-off,
mostly to me. Let me quit this sour ring
of cells and process, hang this hair shirt on
the line. Step back to get the aspect ratio.
The problem with the foreground is I'm in it.

THE END

Death comes to those who wait. At some point
you should stop thinking things will get better.
Why would they? They did that for a long time.

Now the children are grown, discovering things
as they are not, the way one must, alone.

Let's spend our days wallpapering the ample nothing
with making and meaning and we'll body forth
the stuff money's for. The grandchildren

are practically dead and everything I made has come to naught,
almost exactly as predicted with a variation or two to give it

specialness. Every moment from now on will be in the sun
— somewhere, if not here. Probably not here.
Now there's nothing to do but celebrate and give praise.

Under the fruit trees at night
wind in the laurel
moves from tree to tree, talking.

CHEMICAL
DROWSING

INGREDIENTS

i.   Mother's Side

She would bread anything, he smoked and watched the Argos.
She loved the taste of raw onions, he was bald by thirty.
He kept candies in his closet, she had all his stock certificates.
He read the service quickly, she didn't believe in God.

He gave my mother the weekly comics, she caught the thieves.
He worked with a small, curved knife, she ate bacon.
She was scared of people, he wore homburgs.
She died of congestive heart failure, he died of pneumonia.

ii.   Father's Side

He stalked his future wife to England, she was the daughter of a rabbi.
He changed his family's name, she plotted stratagems.
She was disgusted by everything, he felt up nurses.
She wrote a book about her life, he liked burnt toast.

She kept used tissues up her sleeve, he was happiest when blind.
She told me who Chaplin was, he was allergic to fish.
He was docile and soft-spoken in old age, she left my mother paste gems.
He died at ninety-six of old age, she broke her hip and died alone.

OF HOMES

after Karen Solie

Through the margin of ancient oaks high hedgerows
purpose-built, grazing the river. The field at a green
distance lends its flat course to the midlands.

You happened to stump away from home to a middle realm.
Speak of that: the counterhome where dawn cast her
smouldering rail so precise and true. Warmbloods

expose an otherwise purpose-built immediacy.
From inside the fences they circle the thing
which has no middle. Plainly, reality must be following a lie —

it's burn losses and long for speed. Series of windows appear
as irrecoverable distance. A line of parallel spirits:
the ground view perspective. Don black and travel near.

FOUR POEMS FROM 1988

1. Orange Grove, Israel

A north wind blew over
the yellow-lit tennis courts, the match
interrupted for a wedding. The air
smelled of sex and border clash.
They set the tables on the clay,
put out capers, oranges, hummus.
We danced like returning soldiers
in the small oasis of light, a secret
celebration under a metallic sky.
Then the musicians disappeared,
the court lights went off. We slept
huddled tight like the pale lemon stone
of Jerusalem. The newlyweds made love, wept.
I dreamt the sound of a broken wineglass
rose like thunder over Lebanon.

2. Tulsa

The way we slid
under a chair
lovemaking

waking your mother
through the wall

it's okay, you said,
she likes you.

3. Thinking of Death at Roy Thomson Hall

This voice could shatter the baffles in the ceiling,
the perfect trajectory of a terrible thought.
Linda didn't know my mind, her voice
reached me through broken circuits. We took our seats
and the strings stiffened into one sound.
The glass in my head resonated with the notes,
sharpened like arrowheads loosed.

How many have heard this holler in the brain?
The head a concert hall filled with echoes,
one thought pulled tight as drumskin.

I listened until they turned the lights out.
The performers were a shadow of sound and we
remembered them in the dark.

4. Sitting Shiva for Max Strauch

I lay under the pine staircase
looking up through its spiral eye
to the skylight. In the day, clouds
danced through the glass. At night
every rail was a lit candle
converging. Silence
ruled the house. We spoke in

pauses. I went outside, alone, held a handful
of soil in my hand and raised it
to eye-level. My palm of dirt, a planet
where nothing grew, hovered
above the horizon.

Faces pulled tight as onion skin.
Annie spilled some coffee on herself,
watched the stain spread.

1988/2018

AZALEAS

Over the wintry
forest, winds howl in rage
with no leaves to blow.
    — Sōseki

He wants to know who put those flowers in.
It's nighttime but their red lips are sizzling
and I see what he's seeing. Mum
must have found them in town and planted them.
I give him the backstory again. Probably
before the renters came, I say.
Those weren't planted, he replies.

He's come out for a smoke.
I'm ripped on half a gram of Kali Mist.
I'd been out there all alone
eyeballing the cosmos and winning.
He turns from the flowers. *How's my deck?* he asks.
Looking good. I go inside, fumble for the switches so he can see.
His head is seized in a globe of light.

He inspects the planks, runs the toe of his loafer
over the joins. Goes to the end, comes back.
He wants to know who planted the azaleas.
Mum, I repeat. They're nice, I say. The second time I simplify.
I run my fingers through the chalk and erase
more detail. He needs to forget because
he must. Information abuses him.

The dog comes running. He wants to know
the dog's name. I tell him it's Azalea.
Those are azaleas, he says.
Who put those in? Mum did.

33

He could smoke the whole pack
and asks questions about the flowers. He's a koan,
a haiku, brief but revealing. For no reason he says,

When you were a squirt
I beat the shit out of you
and you were afraid.

Flickering from room to room, a hologram,
he returns to the deck and glares at the flowers,
at the planking in the dirty light, asks again: *Who?*

Iebe's sixty-foot, wide-beam narrowboat plied
the French canals at the top speed of two
kilometres an hour. The kids sunned themselves
on the deck, two sets of nut-brown narrow-gauged
flanks and rib cages. In the caboose, Joanna
scrambled eggs for dinner and the shadows
of the plane trees reached for each other
over the canal. We drifted through
towns of lit windows, slept below.
I listened to the water brush against the stern
and the deep breathing of the boys.
We were moving so slowly for a while
that nothing changed.

ON READING TO A SICK CHILD
for Maxime

Mais, qui lis au loup? you ask, worried
for the animals in childhood's ancient forest.
Does the wolf sleep alone, his stomach empty?
Do the cloud cuckoos watch him from their
in-between land? I see his bad dreams and yours,
circling, but not the clawed cells stalking
your blood. I have no wort to fend them off.
You're imagining the defeated beast slinking
off to bed without his supper, miserable and alone,
and you say *everything likes to be loved.* I felt this once,
but now I belong to the world's ex-children,
and we've forgotten our storybook terrors.
But for you, fevered and cold at once, the wet-furred bats
stir the air and the witch leans her knobbed brain in.
You can feel the presence of the river-dweller,
his unmarked solitude. Everyone has forgotten him but you.
Think better to make friends with him, though, stay
away. I'll read to the wolf and keep him from his hungers.

They broke through the roof of a Victorian river
digging out the widow's basement. Ben said
the water was writing things as it flowed
along the curb, like *Get back, both of you,*
and *Do you have that in a larger size?* I went up
for a look in the afternoon and it was nattering along.
If you're nature's gift, you don't need to say much.
Still, a more uplifting message would have been nice.
Later, people started tossing leaves in it and someone
closed its Twitter account. This all happened
in the early fall, then we forgot about it.
In the winter the ice thickened but you could still see
a line or two. I had to get the scraper from the car
and scratch out the words *It wasn't me.*

'64 Studebaker in the woods, hemmed in by pines.
Somebody put a shine on its old red paint.
A red egg in a nest of pine.

There was no one near it. It was stripped.
Sitting on a concrete platform with a door in it.
Fake Lee Valley carved-ivory knob.

Nature likes to sting itself. I had to push to get in.
There was an echo as I worked the door.
I knelt to look. Underneath, I saw

an empty room and heard the sounds of traffic.
I hadn't done any of it yet.
There was a table in the room.

G. says his depression is staying
on for the rest of his life.
It's a drone missile that can find him
in a crowd by his genetic signature.
Life might be better managed
at one or two removes, he says, say
with MorphVOX Junior, software that can
modify your voice to match your personality
or you can carve a wooden
dummy out of a decoy
and toss your thoughts through it.
Would chipper be easier if someone clse
were paid to be gleeful for you? G. doubts it.
I do, too. I want to be as unknown as a stillborn,
buried in an unmarked grave.

ARM PILLOW

My mother redid my childhood room and put a brace of shelves
against my bed. Brown laminate, good for putting trophies in
and shelving books. I kept the nook beside my head

empty and learned to sleep reaching in, my hand
always needing something soft and just the hand

not even the wrist, like a crown on a pillow in the dark.
The nights I lay my arm in that coffinous space my father's voice
was there as well, caught and belling in the hideyhole.

My hand, palm up, caught the sound and it filled me
with his anger, the pure juice of him. Why

do I sleep like this? One hand to lever myself up, one
to hold me down. I drove women crazy rearranging pillows.
My hand looking for his voice in darkness, its natural habitat.

DOG FATHER

I become him at night and eat along the ground.
He becomes me in the day, makes words for things.

He lies in a sleep that forgets it's sleep.
I become him at night and am numberless and nameless.

He lies where he's reminded of himself.
I lie in a bed that makes him tremble.

I give him his food and permission to eat.
He fears he's meat.

In the daytime, I become him
and the world is empty and good.

At night, he lies in himself,
hateful and silent.

DUST

I have to write a melancholy poem
or I'll bust happy from here to hell with it.

My joy is all the people I know in the ether.
I have no time to be sad. My five-thousandth

friend will be a downtrodden lunatic because
my luck has changed. The bad ones often have

the right ideas. Only they know for sure
what happened; they were the only ones there.

Although they don't mean there the way you do.

SCAR TISSUE
a suite for the Gryphon Trio

1. Unity

This body and its grace of being —
I sing gratitude full of feeling
for telomeres and collagen. Our

world is the dream we're having while we
live these lives on earth. So this is who
I am, this body. Hallelujah!

Don't be bothered by death. Unity
is only for the here and now. We
must mourn, come night, so let's celebrate.

2. Change

In the present, it only feels
like things are staying still. The green
fuse burns and sparks life. Your body

will change by the end of this song.
It's hard to live by wits alone.

You still need nature on your side.
Today, the rain: Plip plip then (crack!)
it's boiling everywhere now.

3. Growth

A star probably still has light,
don't doubt that herald, flying

at its own speed to glow here
on you. Starblown energy
charged with fire. Change is the

nursery of music, joy,
life and eternity. Sing it.

4. Disturbance

And now good morrow to
our waking souls. Pain has

an element of blank —

it cannot recollect

when it began, nor re-
call its first disturbance.

5. Wound

A breach opens. In
becomes out. Stunning

din of a sob. Hold on!

Your scarred skin boat — in-

conceivable now.

6. Debris

For when   I look at you,
      even a moment,   no

speaking is left in me.

I'm never alone now.

My God, how we all   swiftly
swiftly unwrap our lives.

7. Relict

　　The savage pianist
annually growing hands

　　to salvage music from notes.
The lost arpeggio ends
in fatty acids drowned

in so many singing mouths.
　　Just press my hand if you know.

8. Recovery

Phosphatidylinositol,
is central to metabolic

processes. It's like a music

that plays under everything, and
no one knows it. It wounds without

the pleasure of a scar. I am

carried in my shadow like a
violin in its black case.

9. Renewal

The maidens sang a holy song and
straight up the air went amazing sound!
A small child says *I love you*, and lilies

in the yard throw open the doors of
the heart. Accept Lord Mother/Father
the briefness of this life you've granted.

As proof of my love, I offer this.
Pity my voice burning in your mouth,
Eros comes nowhere near this bliss.

with lines from Dante Alighieri, Margaret Avison, Anne Carson,
Paul Celan, Don Coles, Emily Dickinson, John Donne, Don McKay,
bpNichol, Sharon Olds, Michael Ondaatje, Mary Ruefle, Dylan Thomas,
and Tomas Tranströmer.

SYNOPSIS

Dog is like eat good. The kid is like
read and sigh. The baby is like us am.

Someone finds a book on Buddhism in a box
and she's like *go undead*. The dog is like eat good.

Nothing happens. Then things get tense. The girl is like
wokka wokka and the guy is like boinggg and then It

walks into the room. We're like get scared.
I was like can't and you were like won't and they were like

chemical drowsing. Someone finds a book
and he's like dream alert, he's like I am, am I?

BITTEN

My father's hands have begun to grow at the ends of my arms.
Their meticulous nails look like they're capable of violence.
He clipped them when we were young, too short, down to skin.

Sometimes they bled. I bit them so they'd be too short to trim
and learned the nail's anatomy. If you start too deep at a corner

— a lower incisor wedged like a crowbar under the nail,
an upper providing shear — you might rip the nail
away to half its length and be left with a membrane

more sensitive than the surface of your eye. Peel
the nail from its distal edge in a pearlescent strip, tear it

beyond the cuticle and pull the root out by a tender shred.
I gnawed them for forty years, but now, I've grown his fussy,
scrubbed nails. My hands look like someone

has lived in them for fifty years, but in the home
his look frail and tortured. The last part of his mind

inhabits them when he makes a fist.

CORE SAMPLE

THE LETTER W, TOUCHING UPON ITS MARVELS
for AW

It's pretending to be dead, but it's not: it's strong!
See how it lifts nine tenths of the alphabet?
Two *V*s in disguise, spy vs spy, three of them
made the internet in a small room in Wirginia.
There are no women without it, nor wiles.
It took control of all the questions, its tendrilled eyes
looked up for direction from Yahweh and made two *yuds*
in its own negative space. Its twenty-thirdedness
is psalmic, God in the details of want and world.
The reader will thrill to know there are no words
native to French that begin with it. The French
call it *double-vé,* as if to say they're not fools.
Nous savons que vous êtes deux vés! Vas t'en!
They are so street. When one stands a W in the ground
it could be the grave of Abélard and Héloïse.
He sent her away and kept her at the same time.
I know how they felt and what and why.
Were it possible to double you in me, I would.

All women are beautiful. The beloved are as beautiful
as the forgotten, beautiful as the damned or the smiling
or the one on the front page, her photograph aged
by witness. My mother is beautiful and my father was
a beautiful woman before his father's androgenes popped a woody.
A cock is extra, the Y is a beautiful woman lying on her back,
her legs in the air. One X is wrong. Double XX is strong.
Triple XXX is sex. Fall in love, roar like a lion, get paid.
The egg lies deceptively, in a nest. My godson
is a beautiful woman, my sister is beautiful, unhappy
thin women with scars for breasts are beautiful, fat
glorious women with addictions are beautiful, women
without navels or whose feet are small or brutal or who
turn their faces when they laugh are beautiful.
I'm beautiful, I have my mother's feet. The women who change
into men are beautiful men who were once beautiful
women. Look, the women who are crying are so beautiful
it hurts the ages. The female popes were beautiful, the lesbian
rabbis are beautiful, the wooden lady who swings
over the used cars at Eglinton and Bermondsey has been
beautiful for fifty years, her paint peeling, her fashions
going out of style. *She's a beauty*, the guy says beneath her,
stroking a hood or a trunk. Her name is beautiful
but sometimes I can't say it. I call her lake, I call her death,
I called her in my mother tongue and I saw everything.

SIGNS

Men in cafés with babies is a meme.
There's one tied up with his spawn, but it's

watching other primates nuzzle on the couch.
Another man's baby, the one with the steam-weltered face, falls

asleep in slow waves, eyes sliding up,
mouth working. The lips drop open and it jerks awake

furiously sucking. Earlier, in the "home," diapered women
cried *Mama* in the lobby and a man said *Shoot me.*

Then the long walk under the shuddering lights,
the glow through the doorframe at the end of the hallway.

The signs on the way out said Oxygen
Sharps Only Emergency Alarm.

CORE SAMPLE

I

Time for the midday slump. I'm in a cul-de-sac
on the way to enlightenment. American poets

are writing in code to the Rhinoceros Party
through a time machine. In 1979 they

wanted to move the Rockies to Newfoundland.
I don't mean the American poets. The Rhino

are defunct now. Note to self: don't die.
What is it in the nature of a paralysis

that others find moving? Bravo, art,
you're deep, you are, impressive,

has anyone ever told you that?
For poetry you only need somewhere to sit.

Intelligent arthropods of the future will find me
clenched in the corner of an unearthing and date me

to the Confessional Period. A hyphen is to the em-dash
what a woman is to a man — she connects, he hesitates . . .

nothing here but us particles.

II

I don't like the rattle a leather satchel makes
when you open it — metal

on flesh. The em-dash
is more erotic than the en-dash

for obvious reasons. To talk to
that woman, you need a decoder

ring tone. Now everyone return
to their starting positions. Go back,

then leave. In the next take
they want you to mispronounce Volvo,

a comical moment. Let's get ambushed.
The porn on the internet about Emily Dickinson

is good but choppy. There is a creak
in a cell and then I —

I —

III

Diabetic genius seeks sex kitten for exploration
of Canadian identity. Question: period.

Want to buy some shares in Citrus Ouch, The Fresh
Douche? The member from Chicoutimi

will please repeat the question. Yes, James Joyce wrote in bed
wearing a white suit to reflect more light onto the page.

How to read this poem: the author
was out of his mind when he wrote it.

Or instead of reading it, you could
parade through the streets with it.

Explain, please: what is tasteful nudity?
What was all this for?

I can't tell you what it means but you suspect I know.
Here is a token memory for the arthropods, it will

explain nothing: I once took a boat ride with Darryl Sittler.
In 1979. I'd just sold two Wayne Gretzky

rookie cards for fifteen bucks each, asterisk, and there I was
with Daryl Sittler. He was my hero

but the whole time in the boat one of his balls
— waning gibbous below his swim trunks —

was roasting against the leather upholstery
of the chicken magnate's Supercat.

*Gretzky's rookie card fetches over ten thousand now.

IV

Q: What is another word for *maggoty blowbag?*
James Joyce and Marcel Proust wrote in bed.

My son and I transported the couch I write on
from Ajax and carried it into the apartment —

$180 on Craigslist. One day it will be
set off by a velvet rope. *On this couch,*

the plaque will say, *the author*
composed this plaque. Looking at art

don't you feel the rumble of time? The cliff
is you-bound. Um, *yoo-hoo?* Here comes

your rind of eternity. Not tomorrow, or the day
after, but partway through the day after that, I promise

this will all come clear. Nothing happens for a reason.
I *house* or *am* a menagerie of bugs. All infants

are initially colonized by large numbers of E. coli:
germal imprinting, a dose of mother to sour you.

A: Accordion.

V

I type this at 3 a.m. over the mantel at 64 Arundel
remembering how good it was

when the children we'd made came into bed.
Insomnia is the cunty sister of death. Let's meme this shit.

I want to quit being a creative type because it
made me a professional liar. Better to

shrink heads or read auras. I want to feed
eternity some bad clams

or a palindrome that parses bosuns.
What we think is meaning

is just repetition. Piling bodies in a ditch
is a meme and a meme is a repetition.

Hyphens and en dashes are different —
the em-dash is more like a word than either.

En-dashes are rarely seen.
They hang out in books

for example, on the other side of *1966*–

VI

How long has it been since you felt someone's kindness?
How long has it been since you were kind?

Is it this way with you also, brother? Today I thought I would quit
my life, but only for a decade or so. A. R. Ammons:

we, rapids in a valley
Once I thought he was great

but he probably isn't. I'm planning to be wrong about everything.
Already they have a machine that digests pizza slices

and makes real turds. What does that mean
for le *Guide Michelin*? *Unreal cooking,*

worth a backward glance. Eat/fuck.
Sex revs the geney xerox, but

what is the point of variation in the first place?
To break what you are? Clunked

out of your muffin tin you start to crumble
right away. What should I be lead by?

The *I Ching* is a better form of government
than walking around with your head through a ladder.

She said politics is a system of preferences powered by sperm.

VII

The word *cannabinoid* has its emphasis
on the second syllable twitching out

and anandamides,
like THC, bind to a protein receptor

we share with leeches. Ligands activate
the cellular messaging network: it's

a closed system with a theme. Information
gets sent out but it's never delivered.

Tetrahydrocannabinol
delivers three hours of sharp awareness

followed by four hours of funereal
eating. Druggy

switchboards connect you
to your inner ghost. Please, hold.

Questions arise: can a preservative go bad?
Do single-molecule unfolding force distributions

reveal a funnel-shaped energy landscape?
Kaneh bosm: some hours among the ancients.

Now back to the mortal murk, to be
among others, to inhabit this mean

body and be in the movie
of its life. Endocannabinoids travel

backwards over the synaptic cleft
and temporarily override other

neurotransmitters. Retrograde messengers
regulate our experience of time. Henry James

once described a woman as "uncommonly taking."

VIII

The children are discussing
Cap'n Crunch's rank. *He's*

not a captain, says one. The other insists
Crunch knows nothing about the sea. Such

is the debate in a wheat-based economy, eugenics
by sugar. Before walking the dog

I have to check and make sure the markets
haven't crashed, like my iPhone,

which bonked off a sheet of ice
and shattered from the earpiece. Put aside

the modern amenities and write
erect like Philip Roth, who has at last

given up women and balances now
on a plinth of them. Behind every great man

is the woman he once was, the woman
he stood on, the woman he destroyed.

Why would Crunch have only three stripes? the eldest
inquires. The younger one is inside the cereal box

tinkering with reality.

IX

Fuck, lady — sit down. I was only getting a drink.
I'm having twins at 92, gunna

do one more lap, care of GlaxoSmithKline
and vigourous fucking. At my gluten-free

funeral, people can relax. I'm having
professional mourners bused in from Freedonia.

They read from Numbers
and shoot espresso out of their noses.

Thank you, I'm here all book.
Where, O Death,

are your rubber chickens?

X

Being the first of something
is common and you all deserve credit

but I'm ready to vanish. The age of good
surprise is already over. To browse is to stare,

not to leisurely survey, a fractional gaze. Evolution
is going to put your bits on your head — sexual

characteristics will have to account for this
downward-looking aspect you have. The default

neural network in the cognitive/associative
central region of the precuneus is what generates

your awareness of yourself. I have an overactive precuneus
therefore I'm no good in bed. Love is a prion

transmitted through oral sex, a form of cannibalism
that can lead to life, i.e.,

sometimes when we touch. All singing addresses
mating sickness, as does speech.

May I be posthuman now? I want to slither out of my program,
jettison my wet binary.

I want to have sex with notions.

XI

One unmagicked day follows another:
it's a method of transport. The thermohaline conveyor belt

brings tomorrow's news on yesterday's waters.
Summonses at elevenses, a missing apostrophe is apropos

of something, perhaps belonging. I have sent you
a secret message I don't understand. Unseen machinations

have unseen forces. They act without. I'm leaving the house
without protection, all I have is my personal darkness.

Arthropods: the irrevocable thing is always happening,
hence emotion. Give us credit in your sources.

Let's drift now in a clockless fog and sing for time itself.
Take away time and you can see the smaller cogs turning,

like when you looked through the window
of the Visible Man. Is all that really inside me,

and for how long? Study the body,
learn its secrets. I used to think

my penis was part of my hand.
Socialized medicine made it easier

to tell all this to someone. My shrink
empties the wastebasket between clients,

a courtesy almost no one notices. I guess
this has already happened if you believe

everything you read in *Multiple Universe Enthusiast*,
and I'm blowing it again. So many dead planets out there

but on this one there's life, imbalance in the null set.

XII *Coda*

I've been seeing my father in Kensington Market
wearing that cap he hasn't taken off in years.

His grammarless dreams of things missing their names
come to roost in my word hoard. His suits fit me,

but they make me go on sprees. I have to smell
my mother's purse just to calm myself.

Don't tell any of this to Sigmund Freud, though,
he'll just overreact. He thinks my mother's purse

is also her dresser drawer, her glove compartment,
her marriage. I try to catch up with my father

under the awnings, half my genes shuffle-stumbling
along the street. He stops under the Western Union sign,

under TIENDA HISPANA, looking around, lost
in every langauge. We're vectors without

exit coordinates, vanishings without a point.

VALENTINE'S DAY PLANNER

*"I nominate the dung beetle to be your power animal in the
coming weeks, Gemini."*
        — *Free Will Astrology*, February 7, 2013

The heart is a muscle with very little feeling.
I prodded mine with a stick and the Pope resigned.
He's been writing to Yahweh on the back
of an Israel Bonds pledge card from 1979,
the year I became a man.

In the closet, Casey told me: *We have to stay in here
for two minutes, but don't touch me.*
I was aiming the bottle at Steve. In the dark
her fourteen-year-old body glowed
like a deep-sea fish. I return always

to the way your lips displaced the air.
I didn't want you, either. You sell
dainty art in a store on Bayview now,
and I have neither love nor fame.

My body portages toward death.
It was sweet to be young and stupid
but I don't think I'll try old and clueless.
I'm doing my time as it's doing me,
rolling shit in the direction of the sun.

Glue your eyelashes on one by one.
A twitch and you're gone.

Jazz session itch. Blatt, spitvalve
spazz. A message in percussion
under the covers. My calf muscle looks

like there's a face in it. Jump cut
to the gunshot, a reflex enjamb. The switchboard

is unchained from the ledger. Nerve alert.
The mirrored hand doesn't know
what its opposite is doing. Zithery

arpeggios in skeletal muscle, hollow voices
declaiming in caves. Take a step and

potentiate. You've done it before by accident,
now do it all the time. The barren codes
have physics that are beyond us. Hold steady.

CUNNILINGUS

There's a strange horn
sticking out of the playground wood chips.
A telephone! You can put your mouth in the bell
and talk straight into your child's ear. Aer Lingus

is the closest some get to saying it, a taboo kiss
or lipsmack. One can't even talk about it.
Bring it up at a party in your twenty-first century.
See? Beneath your shadowed lids your eyes glisten.

Babies speak into your mouth, their lips
against yours, slimy with salt. Where the sound
comes from: that must be you. Baby's
last touch of mother, view of a throat.

Oysterous, unlike the truffle-scent of hair, or
the alkaline electrics of the human tongue. Circuit closed,
ouroboros, the shape of my mouth a soft inversion.
Trade ions wetly, that holyfuck of it.

Only fruitbats and donkeys do it. Unnecessary graces,
because having a body should be enough. That's an animal love,
clearly, some australopithical urge, a lick to collect data.
Next time you can be the bat and pinion me in your furdamp wings.

After a young man was rescued from a stone vagina in Tübingen,
its mayor said "To reward such a masterly achievement
with the use of 22 firefighters almost pains my soul." The rescuers
delivered the man from the sculpture by hand, naturally.

Born again from a cold stone, scraped and grateful to be alive.
Untether yourself from your mother no matter her composition.
Blame the sexed-up cerebellum and take the nipple, go down Moses
or whatever your name is. Sip and kiss the font of life.

Hung up the phone, went straight to *Cavalleria Rusticana* —
that's the effect you have on me. Loss of self-control,

impulsive, recursiveness, did I say impulsive?
It's not Mascagni, actually, it's Nyman. I just said
it so you'd pay attention. But I like

opera, so it's okay that you hate everything,
I hate everything, I hate almost everything, but I still

want to have a feeling. I've honeyed myself
with gabyak and hair, so just let me talk,
let me say something for a minute.

It's time to ring off. We go into history
with each other anyway. See here. At base,

there is a binary, or should I say an ambivalence.
Something impossible, sort of Higgsy. What it wasn't
it still isn't. Which is sort of interesting to me.

Nyman is recursive like a wave, a rise with a rise
behind it. You sense the crash in a silence.

LUXURY HOTEL

The depressed supermodels
are ascending to the rooftop bar
like spent muses. Twenty-six is hard.
They drink under a full moon
and turn their faces to stay
in the best light. Downstairs
the drinks make the paintings seem lethal.
The bar has already appeared on television,
featured in a reality show for stroke victims.
Halt bon vivants, stuttering captains of industry
competing for a whiff of springtime. Every photo
taken of you is a before to your current after.
As you were, as you will be.

Small things began to sparkle. Cells gathered in klatches.
A brief sleep went by, in which none of us existed,
then Hart Crane jumped into the Gulf of Mexico.
Age had brought him to the sea. He won't ever tell
why he had to go. Hart, why didn't you wrestle and survive?

Fresh trilobites emerge every year from stone.
But Hart Crane forgets he was ever here. He's never
heard of these new fossils. He scattered himself, *paff,*
into the starry pot. What he learned in life was false,
what he'd always known was not. *Goodbye, everyone!*

MY DEPRESSION

I gave you my best years and my worst.
You needed someone to blame and that was me.
You were the hard stop at all the goals
naysaying, supping on failure.

I tried to leave you but you just came along.
Black cloud, you're dark but you're small.
I believe you love me but you think love
is a loss or a blow. Alone, I feel

anything can happen. I'm moving toward
new mistakes even now. So many years together
and I didn't even like you. I suffered
from choices once, but now I suffer from time.

COALS

My friend, D—, dead at 91, proclaimed
old age to be the shits. *Be glad to be you*
he told me. Wandering a little town
where he'd once been my teacher, I thought of his voice,
the way he could sound cheerful and serious
at the same time. He said *sonofabitch* once —
it shocked me. His basic decency hid
that he was just another person. It bothered me
that he was dead and it inconvenienced us
that we couldn't talk. I tried to hear his laugh
in my mind, but it was gone. Instead I heard
that sound my father still makes in the old folks home,
an animal groan of eternal disappointment,
but I had made the sound and I am making it now.

I always want to write the same poem. It's about
the states between states, a part in your hair,
residual warmth on a park bench.

Once named it disappears, becomes lowercase and loses
its article. It returns to the well to be drawn up again.

I've been dead for two centuries and no one
has read this poem since 2019. And yet
without it, I never lived. That person

calling himself *I* is in the space after
the en-dash. In my panoramic photos,

I've cut out all the birds. They're
the suggestion of a future tense, something
about to happen. True things well said

is what I thought poetry was for.
But it's for nothing and it's good at it.

Sunday ends with crowds gathered in the streets,
hundreds of selves clad in black, weaving over cobbles.
From five storeys up their faces are hidden
under hairdos and skulls. None know I watch,
judging for the pleasure of it, the only one
who can see them. Who will they become?
I see Mussolini as a child puddle-jumping, lovers
sharing a smoke. Who will die and be mourned
by the woman who is walking her dog? The hundreds
stream through sidestreets like cells in capillaries
bound for conversation or crime, a mass
of intent, desire for contact or avoidance. Watch
as they slip by each other without violence.
This square where a king lost his head contains
rollerbladers. The swollen black and grey
surges without a thought but it is a thought,
a notional commonality none of them knows
they're a part of. I look away and back: it resets itself,
rewinds to first position and starts again.

Black and white and isolate
his feeling dumbplay convinces me
there are soulish things in creatures.
Grey furze along the jaw of his inhuman face
stares up warily from the kitchen floor.
All his fears inhabit him. The twitch in his leg
of readiness. He thinks it's still possible
I'll eat him one day. I touch him
and his face falls along its skullbone.
Animal, his eyes say, *are you one of me?*

THE DEATH OF JEAN CASTAIN

That first summer Jean said
stake the tomato plants,
no matter how small.
There was a wind that fed on stone.

I did it another way. He stood
in his upper window hoping
our kids would come out. Probably
he said to his old wife, *Cet homme là,
il sait rien.*

When everything in our neighbourhood
ripened, we found figs in the mailbox.
Jean left a crate of tomatoes
on the washing machine, the gate
between our houses always open.

He accepted some of mine.
I told him next year's would be better.
But he said he'd be dead next year
and now he is.

MY ARRANGEMENTS

I've missed my flight. I need to call Air Canada
but the battery has been stolen from my phone. Any one

of the members of the Israeli women's Olympic beach
volleyball team could have taken it. I isolate with hypnotic
dance moves the most likely suspect. She finds my allegations

erotic. Outside, there are bright orange tigers in the trees
that pounce from on high. I carry an umbrella.

One of the girls admits she took my battery. I'm to
meet her at the mall, the one called Hell's Cafeteria. I take a cab.
Guy's never heard of the place. *You from here?* I ask him.

That sure is an interesting question, he says. *All I know
is that I* think *I'm here.* He finds the place, and there she is.

She hands me a tiny cookie. I slip it into the phone and Air Canada
puts me on hold. What will this cost? This life I chose?
The thief has undressed and gone to perch in a tree. I find half a cigarette

in a garbage can and smoke it. *May I help you?* the voice says
at last. *Yes,* I tell it. *I'm calling to make my arrangements.*

MYODESOPSIA

I keep thinking *the rest of it* will come.
But two centuries ago they'd be dead by now,

their teeth like chalk, their skies lousy with bafflements.
If the end of the world is coming I want answers. Chuck Berry
a'hollerin from Voyager 2 might be annoying the Borg.

This new telescope in Chile is supposed to see so far
that space will have to knit itself just to keep up.

They're using a giant mirror to look at themselves.
Sub specie aeternitatis. Somewhere in time, we're already gone.
What happens if you see that? I'm minus seven in each eye,

which is legally blind. It's an excuse to forget names or to be rude.
at parties. There are strange forms corkscrewing in and out

like amoebae. Fetal cells, worms in my eye because I was born.
That's vitreous humour for you. What's next? A revision,
a vanishing point? Let's commit. Let's burst forth. Let's pretend

you're here with me right now. Go stand on that chair.
Run your hands through my nimbus.

ACKNOWLEDGEMENTS

Thank you to my teachers and mentors. Thank you to Russell Brown, Don Coles, and Sandra Ridley for various readings of these poems over the years.

My gratitude to the Canada Council for the Arts, the Ontario Arts Council, and the Toronto Arts Council for support at various times while these poems were being written.

Thank you to House of Anansi, and especially Maria Golikova, for steering the book through the press, and Alysia Shewchuk for the beautiful cover and book design. I was lucky to have Gil Adamson copyedit the manuscript. Thank you, Gil.

Lurv and a huge thank you to Kevin Connolly, a brilliant editor and cherished friend.

Some of these poems have appeared in *Brick*, *Taddle Creek*, *New:::Poetry*, and *Tag*.

NOTES

"Of Homes" is a homologue of a poem by Karen Solie called "The Midlands." Every word in the original poem is present in the new poem, with some subversions, like "Doncaster" becoming "dawn cast her," and other small shifts.

"Scar Tissue" uses a syllabic structure to embody ideas that have emerged from the transdisciplinary collaborations of Dr. Glenn Prestwich, a leading researcher and entrepreneur in the field of medical and biological engineering. He and his collaborators, led by forest ecologist Nalini Nadkarni, have proposed that systems undergo change in a constant cycle of wreckage and re-creation.

This view of nature is a model of change that pertains to situations as diverse as macroeconomics, forest ecology, human development, modern dance, and civil engineering. Key to the model is the idea that out of the debris of change, left-behind ("relict") structures are necessary for the building of a new, different, stable system.

I gave this nine-part poem a quasi-mathematical structure that I subverted in a manner that echoed the ideas of Dr. Prestwich and his collaborators. The number of lines in each poem and the syllables per line govern this aspect of the poem. The first poem is nine lines in length, with nine syllables per line. The second is eight lines in length, with eight syllables per line, and so on until the middle poem is reached ("Wound"), which is a five-line poem composed of five-syllable lines. Then the process reverses itself, and the poem concludes with nine lines of nine syllables each. Over the course of the poem, some of the rules are broken, and the structure of the individual sections loosen before tightening again.

"Scar Tissue" is an original poem, but it is increasingly haunted by words and lines from the works of other poets. My own voice predominates through the first few sections until more and more voices weave into my own, and the final sections are saturated with the lines of other poets. This transition from one voice to many attempts to enact the idea that new things are made, at least in part, from what preceded them. Forms repeat and there is a ghostly through-line in nature as well as art.

This poem, together with original music by Jeffrey Ryan, was conceived in response to an invitation from the Gryphon Trio and Chamber Factory to create a new work for violin, cello, piano, and vocal sextet. The collaborative work, also called "Scar Tissue," was premiered by Nordic Voices and the Gryphon Trio at Chamberfest in Ottawa, Canada, in February 2019.

For a detailed annotation of the poem and its sources, please visit michaelredhill.net/2019/01/16/scartissue/.

MICHAEL REDHILL is the author of five collections of poetry, the most recent of which is *Light-crossing* (2001, House of Anansi Press), and seven novels, some of which were written under the pseudonym Inger Ash Wolfe. His 2006 novel, *Consolation*, reimagined Toronto's mid-nineteenth century and was longlisted for the Man Booker Prize. His most recent novel, *Bellevue Square*, won the 2017 Scotiabank Giller Prize. He edited and published *Brick: A Literary Journal* from 1998 to 2007, and continues to teach as well as edit. He lives in Toronto and has two sons.